BASILDON
THEN & NOW
IN COLOUR

JIM REEVE

The
History
Press

First published in 2012

The History Press
The Mill, Brimscombe Port
Stroud, Gloucestershire, GL5 2QG
www.thehistorypress.co.uk

ISBN 978 0 7524 7468 7

Typesetting and origination by The History Press
Printed in India.

CONTENTS

ACKNOWLEDGEMENTS

I would like to thank all the people who have helped me to compile this book, especially the Basildon Heritage Team at Wat Tyler Park, who work tirelessly to collect and preserve the history of Basildon, in particular Jo Cullen, Ken Porter and Denise Rowling, whom I cannot thank enough for their help and patience. They and their team are gathering the history of Basildon and the surrounding districts and, although they would never admit it, are experts in their field: their knowledge of Basildon is boundless. They willingly shared their knowledge and photos of the New Town, and Denise was kind enough to go through the photographs in my book to ensure, as far as possible, their accuracy and was unsparing with her time. Any mistakes are mine. I thank the other members of the Wat Tyler Park team: Tim Cadmies, Sue Ranford, Robin Biddolf and Valerie Hurley, who were very patient with my frequent visits and questions.

Bill Cox's Basildon History Website is a fountain of knowledge and I thank him for allowing me to use material from it. The website is a must for anyone looking at the history of the New Town. Thanks to members of the History Archive for Laindon, Ian Mott, Patricia Mott, Fred Taylor, Mr and Mrs Rudd; Adam Keating of Basildon Council; Vin Harrop, chairman of the Foundation for Essex Art; Gavin Williams, who worked for Yardley for seventeen years and gave me an insight into the workings of the factory and its ultimate demise; Cynthia Earl of Basildon Council.

I wish to thank my friend, neighbour and researcher Mrs Olive Norfolk and my editors at The History Press, Cate Ludlow, Jessica Andrews and Emily Locke. By no means least, I wish to thank my wife Joan, who has kept me on the straight and narrow, taking notes and editing my text. I would also like to thank the many people I have spoken to regarding the book and their contribution towards it.

ABOUT THE AUTHOR

Jim Reeve worked for Basildon Development Corporation – the organisation which was responsible for the design and building of Basildon New Town – for thirty years. Prior to that he did his National Service and then served for five years as a constable in the Metropolitan Police before obtaining a post with the Greater London Council as a Housing Officer.

He is a committee member of the Wickford Community Archive Society and is treasurer of Brentwood Writers' Circle. His previous titles for The History Press include *Wickford Memories*, *Basildon Memories* and *A Schoolboy's War in Cornwall*. He has won various prizes for short stories including Writer of the Year for Basildon, and prizes for essays in competitions run by Essex Age Concern. He is an associate member of the Society of Women Writers and Journalists and was the first man to win a prize in one of their competitions. They started admitting men a few years ago. He loves writing and is fascinated by history, especially local history.

INTRODUCTION

This book sets out to show, as far as possible, some of the changes that have taken place in Basildon over the centuries.

Basildon today is completely different from the small communities that existed during the 1801 census. At that time, Basildon's population was recorded as sixty-two, whereas the more dominant areas of Laindon and Pitsea had populations of 304 and 211 respectively. The population exploded with the advent of the railway stations at Laindon and Pitsea during the late 1880s. Farmers found it difficult to compete with the imports of grain from America and Canada and many were going bankrupt. In 1891 the London Land Co. came up with the idea of purchasing the land from the cash-strapped farmers and selling it on in plots for as little as £10. The scheme was advertised in London, and East-Enders swarmed down on specially hired trains. They were met at the stations of Pitsea and Laindon and taken out to the farms by horse and cart. Before the sale, they were plied with food and copious amounts of alcohol. At first, most of the plots were used for weekends and holidays. For shelter the plotlanders erected tents, caravans, railway carriages – and, in one case, a ship's cabin. It was not long before they started to build more permanent buildings. The population increase encouraged entrepreneurs to open 120 shops in Laindon; there were ninety in Pitsea and Vange, but very few in Basildon.

The Second World War brought the next increase in the population, as Londoners swarmed down to Essex to escape the Blitz. However, even here they were not entirely safe, as the German bombers following the Thames on their way home jettisoned their bombs on the surrounding countryside before crossing the North Sea. Unfortunately, this random bombing killed over twenty people and destroyed 6,000 homes. Twenty-six aircraft were shot down, more Allied than German.

At the end of the war, the Labour Government was faced with a huge housing shortage due to the Blitz. They had to find a solution and, after much debate, brought in the 1946 New Towns Act – and Basildon was born. Industries like Ford's, Ilford's, Yardley's and York Borg were encouraged by grants to set up factories. At first, they brought down their key workers to build up their businesses. The employees were given lodgings so that they could work for the week and return home at weekends. These operatives watched as their future homes were constructed brick by brick. Many of their wives never saw the property until the day they moved in.

The building of the New Towns helped to reduce the lengthy London housing waiting lists. At first conventional building methods were used, but later estates like the Blue House were built using new methods. Soon, however, these houses started cracking up and the under-floor electric heating became too expensive to run. As a Housing Officer in the 1960s, I can remember visiting tenants on the estate: most were using paraffin heaters. After much campaigning by the tenants and some officers, gas central heating was installed. Over the years, the Corporation spent millions of pounds trying to remedy problems. Finally, in the 1990s, Blue House Estate was demolished by Basildon Community Housing Association (now Swan Housing) and the Church View Estate rose from the rubble. I was the Project Manager for this enterprise.

To see more of the town's transformation, I would advise you to visit the historical archive centre at Wat Tyler Park, Laindon and Fryerns libraries and Basildon History Website. These devoted people are collecting pictures and memories of the inhabitants of Basildon for future generations. You may wish to add your own memories of Basildon.

THE PLOTLANDS

THE POSTER BELOW was put up all over the East End of London in 1891 by the London Land Co. At that time Essex farmers were experiencing great hardship in selling their produce – despite the opening of the railway in Laindon and Pitsea, which should have made it easier to transport their produce – as they could not compete with the cheaper grains from Canada and America. The London Land Co. came up with the unique idea of buying up farmland from the cash-strapped farmers and selling it off in plots. They arranged for special excursion trains to Laindon, Pitsea and Wickford. Some Londoners saw it as a chance to escape the slums for a day, while others thought of it as a business venture. Outside the local stations, the horses and carts would wait expectantly for the trains to arrive and when they did the happy, laughing customers would climb aboard and were driven out to the farms where white marquees had been set up with trestles loaded with food and drink. After it was judged that the customers were in the right mood the auctioneer climbed on a farm cart and the sale began. The plots were sold off for as little as £10 each. Those nearest the stations went first and were the dearest.

The new owners would come down by train on a Friday night with tools, timber and tents to stay the weekends. Some would hoist the Union Jack to announce they were there. Soon they were building shacks and installing such things as buses and caravans. They started to cultivate their plots and would return to London on a Sunday night loaded with the fruits of their labours. Some people stayed down for their annual holidays and mothers and children spent the school holidays, with their menfolk joining them at the weekends. During the Second World War many came down to escape the bombing – never to return to the city. A number of plots were never visited and just left untouched. The deeds to the land became lost or their owner died, which caused the legal department of the Basildon Development Corporation many a headache when they tried to sort out the plots' ownership.

THESE HOUSES IN Clay Hill Road were built by conventional methods in the 1960s and therefore have had very few structural problems throughout their lives. Although they were not the first houses to be built, they are typical of the type of house built at that time by Basildon Development Corporation during the early stages of the New Town. Many were let to the key workers of factories that relocated to Basildon from all over Britain.

PLOTLANDS DEVELOPED

THE PHOTOGRAPH SHOWS a typical shack, built by its owners. The plotlanders were a very proud and independent people. At first they had no clean drinking water, gas or electricity. They used filtered rain water, collected on the roofs, until the water company installed standpipes. These used to freeze up in winter. For lighting they used paraffin or candles. For cooking they used open fires or paraffin. Gradually a real community grew up, and they worked together to overcome these problems and built narrow concrete pathways, each wide enough for a pram to go down. They shared the cost of these ventures by each paying an amount a week.

Some people started to live on their plots and travel up to London each day and would cycle down to the train station and leave their bikes unlocked all day. Those without bikes would walk down to the station in their Wellingtons, take them off and leave them there until they returned

that evening. At night, lighted oil lamps were left in the windows of the shacks until the last commuter had passed on his or her way home.

Plotlanders had to think ahead and order their winter coal before October, as the coal carts could not get up the muddy road during the winter months. Doctors left their cars at the bottom of the path and donned Wellingtons to walk up the slippery tracks.

WHEN THE NEW TOWN was proposed under the 1946 New Towns Act there was great opposition, but to no avail – the proposal was forced through. The Basildon Development Corporation was set up and started building the town. They compulsorily purchased the plotlanders' homes but under the law, at that time, they could only pay them the value of the land, which was peanuts; they had to ignore what was on it. This, as you can imagine, caused much bitterness and stress, as I saw when I visited. My heart went out to these people. I am glad to say that the law was later changed, but sadly it was not retrospective.

These independent people were rehoused and given a reduced rent but it did not make up for the loss of their homes. One of the many complaints plotlanders had was that their children did not qualify for all the new homes being built all around them: instead, they had to go on the Basildon Council's housing list.

The picture right shows one of the first houses let in Laindon Hills, with a tenant standing at her front door.

FORTUNE OF WAR

IT IS DIFFICULT to believe that this is the site of the original Fortune of War which, apart from slaking the thirst of the local farmers, was also an inn. It has stood proudly on the same ground at Noak Hill Road since 1800. There is some controversy over how it obtained its name: some believe it was named by a British soldier returning from the Napoleonic Wars, while another school of thought maintains that it was named after a 'Fortune Fair', which was held in a nearby field every year. It is difficult to establish which is right, but the building has stood the test of time. It was included in an auction held in Chelmsford on 30 January 1830 along with a number of other inns from the district. At the turn of the twentieth century it was falling into disrepair and a major reconstruction was undertaken. (© *Basildon History Site*)

THE OLD FORTUNE of War in 2012. Its death knell, as a public house, came when the new Southend Road was opened in 1925 by Prince Henry, son of King George V, and with the advent of works' outings to Southend to see the lights. It struggled on for a few years by selling alcohol to local farmers while they waited for the local forge to carry out repairs to wheels or shoe horses. In 1928 it was no longer economically viable and, like many public houses today, it ceased trading. The building was sold and converted into a printing works: this traded for many years until it was sold to DGT, who sell tyres and alloy wheels.

The building still maintains its old dignity and stands out like a sentry, guarding the road from Billericay to Basildon.

THE NEW
FORTUNE OF WAR

ANXIOUS TO CATCH the passing trade on its way to the seaside resort of Southend, The Hustler opened in 1928 on the A127 and soon became a popular comfort break. Within a year the owners had changed the name to the Fortune of War.

During the Second World War the Home Guard met up in the public house and drilled in the grounds. They also had a gun entrenchment on the roundabout, surrounded by barbed wire. Just before D-Day, John Rudd remembers the road being closed and army lorries and troops ranged along the road. He got quite friendly with them, and the troops would give him sweets. Then, one day, they were gone – D-Day had begun.

Before and after the war, the public house was very popular as a watering hole for firms' 'beanos', which were all the rage at that time. The staff of London public houses, especially in the East End, also organised outings to see the lights in Southend during September and October. I remember, as

a boy of nine, standing outside The Standard Public House in Hackney waiting for the coaches to start off on their annual outing. As they moved off, the day-trippers would open the windows and throw handfuls of coins out to us youngsters. They bounced on the road and a dozen scruffy East-End children would scramble for them, laughing and giggling.

I can also remember, as a boy, cycling the 64-mile round trip to Southend and stopping at the Fortune of War for refreshments (my own, of course – I was only twelve!). Also, I will never forget how hard I found it to sit down for the next week...

IN 1983, THE public house owners changed the name to The Hustler again, hoping that it would revive the business. However, in 1985 they changed the name back to the Fortune of War. By 2003 it became evident that the public house was becoming uneconomical and Mitchells & Butlers, the owners, put the site up for development. Before the public house was demolished a thriving blues club used to meet there: it had over 600 members. When the building was razed to the ground the club moved to Barleylands.

On 23 August 2003, the Fortune of War closed; Barratt's, the builders, redeveloped the site and sold the houses. They called the cul-de-sac Walnut Close. The roundabout, however, is still referred to as the Fortune of War.

THE PRINCE
OF WALES

THE PRINCE OF WALES public house in the 1920s. It was
built in the seventeenth century and has changed hands many
times since then. Punch Taverns owned it until recently, when
it was sold to Spirit Public Houses. When much of Basildon
was farmland, it was a favourite watering hole for farmers
and their workers. Note that there are no women in the
photograph: it was taken at a time when it was frowned upon
for a woman to enter a public house alone.

THE PRINCE OF WALES in 2012. It is still a favourite drinking
place. Whereas in years gone by public houses rarely sold
food, the Prince of Wales now serves good food to the local
population, especially to workers from the industrial estate and
Basildon town centre, who want to get away for a quiet meal

during their lunch break. Before the Second World War this was the starting point for a race involving four public houses: the Prince of Wales, the Fortune of War, Laindon Hotel and The Crown. Each team consisted of four men who pulled a cart from pub to pub, stopping at each one for a drink. Finally, they staggered up the hill to The Crown at Laindon Hills, pulling their carts behind them, no doubt very much the worse for wear!

ENEFER'S CAFÉ

IN 1953 MR and Mrs Christensen took over Enefer's Café on the Southend Arterial Road, opposite the Fortune of War. In those days, works' outings were very popular. Coaches would take a comfort break on their way to Southend in the morning and then again on the way back home – by which time many of the customers would be two sheets to the wind! The café stayed open until the early hours of the morning to capture the returning revellers. I was told by the owners that the revellers caused a lot of damage on the way back and staff had to be very vigilant.

To give the reader some idea of how busy the café was, they provided 1,000 rolls each day; in a shed at the back they made buckets of ice-cream. The traffic increased during September and October when people streamed down to see the lights at Southend. The illuminations attracted thousands of visitors each night. Different coloured lights were strung along the front, each of which flashed on and off. Clowns, butterflies, flags and every type of image appeared and disappeared. On the embankment overlooking the sea was a fairyland of elves, fairies, pixies and enchanted castles – all the fairy stories from one's childhood. As a child, I stood mesmerized.

SADLY, ENEFER'S CAFÉ has long gone. It was replaced with a Happy Eater during the 1980s. This was subsequently replaced by a McDonald's. The stop is still busy. However, since Southend no longer has the lights, the day-trippers have ceased to come in droves as they used to do – but Southend still has its attractions, with its sandy beaches and its 1.5-mile pier stretching out to sea.

THE OLD FORGE

THE OLD FORGE in Lower Dunton Road. This picture was taken in 1920. The forge was built in the 1800s. During those very early days it was owned by a family called Newman. At that time the area was mostly farmland, as can be seen by the number of cartwheels leaning against the walls. Before the present owner's father bought it in 1968, the building was used by the Gas Board. (© Newmans)

THE OLD FORGE in 2012. Some things in Basildon never change, and the Old Forge in Dunton Road is one of them: apart from a small extension at the rear of the property, it looks much the same. Note that instead of wheels and farm implements leaning against the wall there are wheelbarrows, rakes and garden tools, giving an indication of the change in the area, which today is mainly residential. The business will be in safe hands, as the owner's fourteen-year-old son will be joining the firm directly after he leaves school and already has the makings of a skilled craftsman. The forge is fascinating: stepping inside is like stepping back in time as the furnace roars, throwing out heat that stings one's face. All around are rakes, shovels, wheelbarrows and pieces of beautiful, ornate ironwork. Mr Quelch's skills are in great demand, he having carried out work for many of the great houses in London.

SOUTHEND
ARTERIAL ROAD

THE PICTURE SHOWS the A127 Southend Arterial Road in the 1930s. It was opened in 1925 by Prince Henry, son of King George V, but it was not converted into a dual carriageway until 1936. It was the era of the works and club outings and Southend was a very popular destination, especially during September and October, when the road buzzed with traffic of all types on its way to see the lights.

THE A127 SOUTHEND Arterial Road in January 2012, showing the present dual carriageway. Note how the volume of traffic has increased. Southend is still a popular destination for family days out though alas, the lights are no longer turned on in September. Gone also is the cycle track that used to run the length of the road. Before and shortly after the Second World War, this was crowded with cyclists. As a twelve year old, I can remember a gang of us from the East End following the cycle track safely all the way to Southend.

THE RADION CINEMA

THE RADION CINEMA, also known as the Laindon Picture Theatre. It changed its programme frequently, as in the days before television most people went to the pictures at least twice a week. It could hold 500 patrons. Mr and Mrs Silverman ran it, with the help of their daughter. Many of Laindon's senior citizens remember Saturday morning pictures, when they were shown such films as *Tarzan*, Laurel and Hardy pictures and serials featuring Tom Mix – at the end of each episode, it seemed, our hero's coach would be heading towards a cliff edge and certain death, but in the following week's opening scene he would jump out of the stagecoach just as it went over the cliff. Alas, the Basildon Development Corporation wanted to widen the road and the last film, *Wait Until Dark*, was shown on 3 February 1969. For the rest of 1969 the

cinema was used as a bingo hall, but it was finally demolished later that year. The seats were not wasted, but were put to good use in the new Towngate Theatre.

IT IS FITTING that, in 2012, the Laindon Library stands on the site that was once the cinema, for as well as lending books it has computers that give customers free access to the world of the Internet. The Laindon Archive Society meets there once a month, collecting and recording people's photographs and memories of the area for posterity. They have a fine collection of memorabilia and a website, which is well worth a visit.

LAINDON HIGH ROAD

LAINDON HIGH ROAD during the 1920s. The changes that have taken place are almost impossible to take in. When this picture was taken there were 120 shops between Laindon Station and the Fortune of War, selling everything from shoes to perfume. However, once the town centre was built in the 1960s the shops were moved there and the High Road slowly died. The final blow came when the Laindon Shopping Centre was built in the 1960s. Shops like Collings' moved to the new location. However, nothing seems to stand still in Basildon, and now the centre is again being redeveloped. *(Courtesy of Basildon Heritage Museum)*

LAINDON HIGH ROAD in 2012. Most of the 120 shops that once graced the High Road have now gone. Only a few, down near the station and by the Fortune of War, remain. None can be seen from the bridge that now spans the dual carriageway. Danacre is on the right of the

picture and is one of the entrances into Laindon Shopping Centre. The Laindon Shopping Centre, which once thronged with customers, was opened in 1969. The dominant feature of the centre was an office block called Clock House which, as the name implied, had a large clock that used to ring out every quarter of an hour. In the block were a number of businesses including Steggles Palmer, a solicitor's, an insurance company and, on the ground floor, the Basildon Development Corporation's housing office, which managed the 6,000 properties in the Laindon area. In the shopping centre there was a Barclay's Bank, a library, a post office, Peachey's, a greengrocer's, and many other shops. The Joker public house is one which is still there today. Under the shopping centre is a large area which allows the shops to be supplied out of sight. The centre was sold by the Corporation to a private buyer in 1972. The once busy shopping area began to fall into disrepair and a decision was made in 2008 to refurbish it. The office block was demolished and along with it went the clock, which has been put into storage.

NORTHUMBERLAND AVENUE

NORTHUMBERLAND AVENUE IS on the left of Laindon Station. The picture shows the area as it was in the 1920s and 1930s. It is now mainly taken up with housing built by the Basildon Development Corporation during the late 1970s, and it is difficult to visualise it as it was in its heyday, teeming with activity. In the foreground are the premises of Churchill and Johnson, timber and builders' merchants, who had yards in other parts of the town too.

THE WINSTON CLUB can be seen in the background and was set up as a working men's club. Originally it was called the Windsor Club but in 1940 the name was changed to the very popular

war leader, Churchill. In the early days they ran beano outings and also had a Christmas club into which members put so much a week for Christmas. Contributors could have a small loan for emergencies during the year. This was a great help to poor families during the festive season. The club would have concerts, where one of the locals would play the piano and people would gather round and sing songs. There was always a Christmas party for the children and members played darts, dominoes and cards. Today, it is still a thriving social club but its activities have been updated.

The houses are in Oxcroft and at one time the tenants were up in arms because of commuters going up to London parking their cars in the road. Sensibly there are now parking restrictions to prevent this.

HIAWATHA HOUSE

WHEN THIS HOUSE was built Mr Foulger, the owner, called it Greenhaugh. However, because of its tower the locals soon nicknamed it 'Hiawatha House'. It stood on the junction of Laindon High Road and St Nicholas Lane, and was for many years a doctors' surgery. In 1963 Dr Millwood joined Dr Long in the practice. Many of the patients lived on the plotlands and so, when the doctors visited, they took their Wellington boots with them. When Blue House Estate was built in the 1960s the surgery moved to Danacre and later, in the 1980s, the practice was moved to the purpose-built Laindon Heath Clinic, which still serves the community today.

WHEN HIAWATHA HOUSE was demolished a Roman Catholic church was built on the site, though this later moved to a new building in Florence Road. Basildon Community Housing Association (now Swan Housing Association) took it over in the 1990s and renamed it Morris House, after its first chairman, Phil Morris. This was the second office of Basildon Community Housing, the first being in Clayhill Road, Vange. Swan Housing took over in the region of 2,000 properties from the Commission for New Towns after tenants voted which organisation they wished to be managed by (Basildon Council or Basildon Community Housing Association). The only exception to the transfer was the Blue House Estate, which was transferred automatically to the Housing Association for the redevelopment of the 800 properties.

LAINDON
RAILWAY
STATION

THIS PHOTOGRAPH SHOWS the funeral of Station Master Harvey, who ran this station for many years.

The famous actress Joan Sims was born in the station master's house on 9 May 1930. Her father was then the station master. She lived there until 1952. She was educated in St John's School, Billericay, and then went on to Brentwood County High. She started her acting career, like many actors, in a local drama group, the Laindon Players. It is said that she often entertained passengers waiting for trains with impromptu routines on the platforms. During her long career Joan acted in

many roles, but she is best known for parts in the *Carry On* films. Joan died on 28 June 2001, aged seventy-one. A blue plaque commemorating her life was unveiled on 9 May 2009 and can be seen on the station wall.

Basildon town centre did not have a rail station until 25 November 1974. Travellers near the town centre had to travel to Laindon or Pitsea stations by bus in order to catch a train. It now takes thirty-nine minutes to travel to London.

THIS PHOTOGRAPH SHOWS Laindon Station in 2012. It does not seem to have changed much. There are now three platforms joined by a bridge, and instead of a ticket collector there are barriers. Nearly 2 million passengers use the station every year.

LAINDON HOTEL

THE LAINDON HOTEL on Laindon High Road was built in 1896 and was owned by Seabrooks & Sons. This picture shows it when it was at its height, in the 1920s and 1930s. I understand that it was once proposed that a racecourse be built near the hotel: the jockeys were going to live in Strickland, in Helmore Crescent. Unfortunately, however, the racecourse never did materialize: if it had, perhaps the Laindon Hotel would not have closed. The ground behind the public house was used for a long time as a football pitch, on which the Berry Boys and the hotel's own team used to play.

IN 1967 CHARRINGTONS took over the public house, and it remained a popular venue for the local population. During the 1970s it was renamed The Laindon and classified as a Grade II listed building. Sadly, however, it gradually fell into decline. It closed in the 1980s and lay empty for a number of years. Then it was subjected to a number of arson attacks, which made the

building vulnerable to vandalism. Finally, in 1991, the once-proud hotel was demolished. The land is owned by Ind Coope Brewery.

This photograph, taken in 2012, shows the now-desolate site of the hotel, which has become a dumping ground since the building was demolished. The good news is that, after thirteen years, Laindon Holdings have applied for planning permission to build a KFC restaurant here, with 331 metres of floor space, parking space and a drive-through service.

LEE CHAPEL NORTH

LEE CHAPEL NORTH in 1960, before the site was developed. Most of the homes were bungalows, but they did have electricity – one in this photograph even has television. The Basildon Corporation compulsorily purchased such properties for what we would consider today to be 'peanuts'. They paid only for the land and ignored anything that was on it. It was not the Corporation's fault, as they could apply the law only as it stood under the 1946 Acquisition Act. After much campaigning and heartache, this unfair law was finally changed in 1965. Tragically, however, for most of the plot-holders it was too late.

LEE CHAPEL NORTH in 2012. This area of housing was built by the Basildon Development Corporation using conventional methods and therefore there have been very few construction problems over the years. This and Lee Chapel South are some of the most desirable areas in Basildon. Many of the houses are now in private hands following the sale of council properties under the 1980 Housing Act. When the properties were first built, Basildon Development Corporation was quite strict about the appearance of the houses. Tenants were not allowed to park on the open-plan front gardens. They could not carry out any improvements without permission – which was often refused. They could only erect television aerials at the rear of the properties so that they could not be seen. Many members of the housing profession, including myself, felt tenants should be able to carry out alterations to the properties. It was argued that they would then take a greater pride in their homes. Eventually, an Act of Parliament changed all that and finally tenants where allowed to carry out alterations, subject to supervision. In 1979 the population of Basildon was 11,238.

VANGE WELL, No. 5

THIS PICTURE SHOWS Vange Well No. 5, which was once a mineral well and can be located on the outskirts of Martinhole Wood, Langdon Hills. The structure looks as if it was designed in the style of a Greek temple, and could have been called beautiful in the past, but time has taken its toll. It is a pity that this once proud building, which stood in the open, is now hidden by trees, where nature is gradually taking its course.

In the 1900s, Mr King, a farmer, depended on well water to drink and give his animals. During one hot summer the well dried up, so he dug another. When he tried the water from the new well, however, he found it had a funny taste. When boiled, it left white sediment in the bottom of the kettle. He had no option but to give the funny-tasting water to his cows – and, to his surprise,

they thrived and gave more milk. Soon, the local villagers heard about the magic water and started drinking it. The national press took up the story, and soon crowds came down to drink the water. Edwin Cash, who was a London publican, owned land next to Mr King's, dug his own well, and had the water analysed. He found that it did have medicinal qualities: it was considered to cure stomach problems, lumbago, rickets and certain nervous complaints. Being a businessman, he saw the potential to make money and dug five wells. He started bottling the water, and orders came in from all over the country. To attract buyers, Edwin erected a notice directing customers from the Five Bells Public House to his farm, which was advertised as 'The Magic Well in the Vale of Health'.

The Vange Water Co., as Cash called it, stepped up their marketing strategy in the 1920s, when they labelled it 'Farmer Cash's Medicinal Vange Water', priced at 2s 3d. For a few years the business flourished but then, in 1927, a tuberculosis hospital was built nearby. Locals suspected that it did, or might, contaminate the water, and as a result the business gradually closed. (© Thomas Barnes)

THE BUILDING IS now a wreck and is gradually falling down. It is badly cracked and the plaster needs replacing. However, it would cost thousands to renovate. Hidden away in the undergrowth there can still be found evidence of the other four wells. If one looks hard enough, one can find the concrete hard-standing on which stood a wooden hut. In it, Vange Water Co. bottled and stored their health-giving water.

PARKINSON BROTHERS

THE PARKINSON BROTHERS – Cliff, Bert and Cyril – ran a garage on the north corner of Somerset Road and Laindon High Road. The family lived in Cottenham House which was also in Laindon High Road. Their father, James, served in the army in the First World War and soon after he was demobbed he opened the business. They had to pump the petrol by hand, as like most premises at that time they did not have electricity. The firm became an integral part of the community, selling paraffin for lighting and heating, running a taxi service, and hiring out cars for weddings.

Bert branched out on his own: he opened a garage on the Southend Road, opposite the Fortune of War. He was well known for having an old Douglas motorbike which was driven by a leather belt. He and his friends used to race the bike down the A127 at breakneck speeds: it is said they even reached 70mph, though without a speedometer they could not be sure of this.

During the Second World War the firm employed Bernard Biggs as a car mechanic, and when trade was slack he moonlighted and drove buses for Eastern National.

WHEN THEY WERE compulsorily purchased in 1960, the business was forced to move to Durham Road. After a time the business evolved, and mainly dealt in bicycles; the brothers were renowned for their skill in repairs. They continued trading right up to the 1990s. The corner is now called Parkinson's Corner, in honour of Cliff Parkinson.

Cliff Parkinson was the youngest of the three brothers. He never went to school and was educated at home. At seventeen he joined the firm and devoted the rest of his life to it. He never married, but towards the end of his life he started going on holidays abroad – and regretted that he had not done so sooner. This much-loved Laindon character, who never suffered fools gladly, sadly died, at the age of ninety, on 24 November 2004.

Here is Parkinson's Corner in 2012. It is surprising to note that the current shopping parade still retains much of its old look even though Parkinson's is no longer there, with shops like Rose Buds, Robert Lewis's accountants, Zade and Ale's Art.

WELCOME CAFÉ

THIS PICTURE SHOWS the Welcome Café, Charsley's Shoes and Simmons' Corn Chandlers, Laindon High Road, during the 1930s; three of the many victims of the new town centre and Laindon Shopping Centre development. During this time there were 120 shops along the Laindon High Road.

This street used to be called 'the church mile' because of the number of different religious denominations found along it. During the 1800s there were only three churches in Laindon: St Nicholas on the hill, St Mary's and the old parish church in Dunton. When the plotlands opened up in the 1890s, many East-Enders came to

the area: as they did not generally like orthodox churches, they opened the less formal Baptist and Methodist churches, and other religious groups followed suit.

LAINDON POLICE STATION now occupies the site. It was built during the late 1980s. It is a very busy station which deals with the whole of the Laindon area. The police attend the Joint Estate Meetings which are held on a regular basis and make a very valuable contribution to the community.

COLLINGS'

IN THE EARLY twentieth century Mr Collings set up businesses on the corner of Windsor Road. They occupied Nos 1 and 3 Laindon High Road. He had four shops, one for each of his daughters. The shops dealt in everything from drapery, hardware, haberdashery and toys to electrical goods and stationery. When Basildon Corporation built the Laindon Centre during the late 1960s, Mr Collings knew he would be compulsorily purchased and so relocated all his businesses to the centre. He traded there for many years until the centre started to decline. Mr Collings died in the 1990s.

When Collings' shop was at its height it had lawnmowers, rakes and garden implements stacked outside. The Basildon Development Corporation's Area Housing Office was nearby, and I can remember on a number of occasions hearing a rattle of a lawnmower and the cries of 'Stop thief!' as a shop assistant tried to catch a shoplifter who was towing a mower behind him.

THE LAINDON COMMUNITY CENTRE 2012 is now approximately on the site of Commercial House. It has a sports hall, three badminton courts, a bar and a gym. A number of clubs use the facility, from bee-keeping to kung fu. It can be hired for weddings and functions. Off the picture on the right is Somerset Road: this is where Basildon Community Housing Association (now Swan Housing) built the first houses to decamp the Blue House Estate, now Church View, in the 1990s.

BOONS
AND LING'S

BOONS AND LING'S during the 1930s were located in the North Parade stores. This area was situated just past St Nicolas Lane, just to the right of Swan Housing Association's Morris House.

Boons was a newsagent's. Patrick Neville did a paper round for them during the 1960s and remembers trudging through the muddy, unmade roads with his bag slung over his shoulder, trying to resist peeking at the *Dandy* and *Beano*. Along the same parade of shops was Grey's Co-Op and a haberdashery shop called Moorcroft, which was owned by Miss Butler.

Ling's was owed by Hatheralls, who sold toys, dolls' prams, cycles, sporting goods and anything to do with sports. At Christmas, parents would take their excited children to see Father Christmas in his grotto. After

sitting on his knee and telling him what they wanted, they would go away tightly clutching a toy. The Employment Offices were opposite the road where Danace stands today. There was also an off-licence named The Challenger. The closure of these shops was a pity, but they were the victims of the town centre and of Laindon Shopping Centre.

WILLOW COURT, OWNED by The Guinness Trust, was built on the site of Boons and Ling's. To the right of the flats is an underpass, which gives an indication of how busy the road is today. Further towards the High Road is Swan House, which appears to be going through another transformation: it currently has fencing around it.

OLD LAINDON LABOUR EXCHANGE

THE OLD LAINDON Labour Exchange was opposite Manor Road. The site had been used before as a clothing factory that employed many of the women from Basildon. During the 1950s it had been home to Baigents, the printers. The Exchange served the population and dealt with all unemployment matters until its closure in the 1970s, when the office was transferred to the town centre. Unemployment benefit came in during 1911, but by 1921 there were 2 million unemployed claiming benefit. After the Second World War the Government promised full employment, and during the 1950s the percentage of unemployment was only 3 per cent of those eligible to work. The labour exchanges in Basildon were lucky – they had factories like Ford's, Carreras' and Yardley's, who had set up factories in the New Town and had helped to keep unemployment lower.

UNFORTUNATELY, THEY COULD not shield local workers during the oil crisis of 1973 and 1979, when we had the three-day week. I can remember sitting in the housing office trying to work by the light of a candle. Danacre Flats were built approximately on the site of the old employment offices and were part of the old Blue House Estate – but did not come under the Church View development, much to the consternation of the tenants.

The doctors' surgery moved here from Hiawatha House to a ground-floor flat in Danacre when the flats were built, but once the new clinic on the edge of the Blue House Estate (now Church View) was built, the doctors moved there. A dentist took over the lease of the premises.

DRY STREET POST OFFICE

DRY STREET POST OFFICE during the 1930s and 1940s. This property was originally called the Red Cow Beer House. During the 1930s it became a post office and served the local farms and surrounding community in the days when postage was a few pence and there were at least two deliveries a day. At one time the property had a thatched roof. Dry Street seems as if it has avoided the encroachment of the New Town, and it is difficult to believe that not far away lies the built-up area of Basildon.

But a dark shadow hangs over the meadow to the north of Dry Street: it was proposed, some twelve years ago, to build 1,300 houses on the site. Thanks to strong opposition the plans were thrown out – but I understand there is talk of building a new college.

At the top of the street stands The Crown public house and opposite is the cricket field where, on a summer's evening, can be heard the very English sound of leather on willow. *(Both old pictures courtesy of Basildon Heritage Museum)*

TODAY THE POST OFFICE is a dwelling house. The road leads up to Langdon Hills Country Park. The park is ancient and goes back to before Saxon times. Its name means 'Long Hill'. It is 385ft high and overlooks the Thames, which dispels the popular myth that Essex is flat. In 1886 it housed brickworks (with two kilns) in the place where the toilets are today. There was also a light railway to bring the clay for the bricks and to take them away.

TRANSPORT
IN THE AREA

AT THE TIME of the advent of the railway stations in Pitsea and Laindon in 1886 and 1888, respectively, horse buses were the norm. Tom Webster started his Motor Service in 1920 and was soon running buses from Laindon Station, via Brentwood, to Romford. The return fare was 1*s* 2*d*. It cost 1*d* from Laindon Station to the Fortune of War. The first bus was not until 10 a.m. and the last bus was at 6 p.m. On Saturdays the buses to Brentwood ran much later. As the business expanded, he employed his two sons, Dick and Tom. In 1936 he sold his eight buses to New Express Saloons, who operated the City Services. Tom died in 1963. His sons continued to operate excursions, but the company finally had its last trip in 1971.

At about the same time as Tom set up his business, Fred Hinton opened Hinton's Laindon & District Motor Services, running a double-decker, open-topped bus from Laindon Station to Wash Road. The Campbell family started running a single-decker bus from Pitsea. The seats were wooden and in the 1940s, as a young boy, I can vouch for the fact that they were very hard and uncomfortable

to sit on! The buses had a crew of two, a driver and a conductor. The conductor (or clippie) collected the fares and punched the tickets.

FROM THE 1930S to the 1950s, the City Coach Co. ran a number of local buses and operated services to Brentwood, Billericay and Wickford. The Eastern National Omnibus Co. started a service in Basildon to the new developments. In 1951 they opened a bus garage in Clay Hill Road. However, with seventy buses in the fleet the garage was too small and so they built a new one in Cherrydown. The old station was demolished and a neighbourhood shopping centre was opened on the site. During 1958 the new bus station in Southernhay was opened and buses extended their routes to take in new parts of Basildon that had been built at that time. The bus stop in Southernhay consisted of a double island. In 1966 the bus station was rebuilt and turned into one bay. When the local services were deregulated the routes were taken over by First Thamesway, Jacksons and Nelson's Independent.

ST NICHOLAS' CHURCH

ST NICHOLAS' CHURCH dominates the surrounding countryside and can be seen from the Southend Road. It is said to date back to the twelfth century. Its church register goes back as far as the sixteenth century and there are claims that some of its timber came from ships that were engaged in the Spanish Armada.

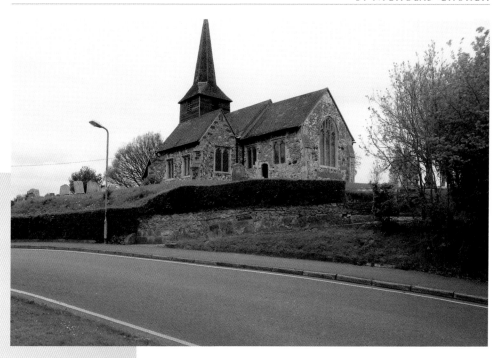

John Puckle set up a school in what is known as the priest house, at the rear of the church, in 1778 and in his will left his farm to St Nicholas' church to finance it. There is a tablet in the church recording this fact.

The first headmaster, it is believed, was Hugo Peters. He was hung, drawn and quartered by Charles II, when he took the throne, for siding with Oliver Cromwell. One teacher, James Mathews, taught at the school for over thirty years from 1778. When he died he was buried in the churchyard. The last teacher was James Hornsby, who taught at the school for forty-eight years. He outlived his three wives and died in 1887. He is also buried in the churchyard – as are his three wives.

During the Second World War a flying bomb landed nearby, which shook up some of the local population. Luckily no one was killed or injured, though the bomb did damage the church. St Nicholas' church gave its name to the Church View Estate, built in the 1990s.

THE OLD CLASSROOM can still be seen today and there is talk of the Revd Diane Ricketts setting up a heritage centre so that children of today can experience what school was like in years gone by. After all the centuries the church has seen it still stands, proudly surveying Laindon and all the changes that have taken place. If only it could speak and reveal its secrets!

ILFORD'S

ILFORD PHOTOGRAPHIC COMPANY started trading in Ilford, Essex, in 1879. Its beginnings were humble as the owner, Mr Harman, set up his business in the basement of his house on the corner of Cranbrook Road, Ilford. As business expanded they moved to Roden Street, Ilford, but they soon outgrew these premises and they started to branch out to different parts of the country, where they set up factories.

Each of these seemed to specialize in some aspect of photography. In 1957 they moved from Brentwood; many of the Brentwood staff complained of the lack of heating, not knowing that a move to Basildon was imminent and the management had to keep the cost down. After the move they were able to take advantage of the cheaper rents offered by Basildon Development Corporation and the pool of labour in the New Town. They set up the factory in Christopher Martin Road and Paycocke Road on the industrial site. Here they specialized in colour films and transparencies, which were, at that time, in their infancies. Ilford's trademark was a paddle steamer, which was registered as far back as 1897 and remained unchanged for sixty years. The factory had its own magazine and was very paternal, as were most of the factories at that time. Most had their own social club, football and cricket teams. *(Courtesy of Basildon Heritage Museum)*

AS DIGITAL CAMERAS and computers came in, there was no longer the need for a processing plant, and so Ilford's closed their factory in Basildon. The name still exists, however, as the factory that once processed most of Ilford's colour films has been converted into small units and is today called Ilford Industrial Site. The units house every type of business, from engineering, carpentry and storage to computer firms.

PITSEA STATION

PITSEA STATION WAS authorised by Act of Parliament in 1882 creating a more direct line from Barking to Pitsea. The station opened about the same time as Laindon Station, in 1888. The contractors had problems with subsidence at Dunton, and therefore when trains went through Pitsea they had to slow down. For many years Pitsea Station was called Pitsea Junction. The line cut the distance to travel to London by 8 miles, thereby saving time. The London and Blackwall leased the line to Betts for twenty-one years. Tilbury and Southend Co. took it over in 1912 and ran it until Midland Rail took over. In 1923 it came under LMS. Today it is franchised to the National Express group.

The line was not without accidents, and in 1961 a train came off the rails between Laindon and Pitsea, killing one person and injuring many more. A subsequent enquiry blamed one of the railway workers.

The photograph opposite captures the final days of steam in the Thames Valley, in the 1950s. *(Courtesy of Ben Brooksbank, CC BY-SA 2.0)*

PITSEA STATION TODAY. At first the trains were steam-powered. Then, in 1962, the railway installed overhead electric cables – though it only used them during off-peak times. Finally, after a century, the last steam train passed over the lines. In 1971 the station was refurbished. A single-storey entrance was installed, with a ticket hall.

PITSEA POLICE STATION, RECTORY ROAD

RECTORY ROAD IS one of the oldest and most important roads in Basildon. In days gone by it appears to have been tranquil and quiet until development started in the 1950s. At one time it ran from Burnt Mills Road to the old A13. During the 1970s the road was altered and a large roundabout built, which was part of the planning for the new housing estate at Felmores and Tyefields. The picture shows the old police station from which the whole of Pitsea was patrolled, initially on bicycle, foot and horse but with the advent of time – and to keep up with the criminals

– later by car. As at most police stations the officers here still patrol on foot, though. The station was closed in 1967 and Pitsea had a temporary station till the new one was built in 2000.

The main centre of Pitsea is further down, past Howard Park and to the right in Pitsea High Street. Note the single car and cyclist. *(Courtesy of Basildon Heritage Museum)*

THE NEW POLICE STATION was built in 2000. Note the number of police cars outside the station. I wonder if it is the same cyclist? Rectory Road is very different today, as traffic streams on its way to Pitsea and the A13 and gives an indication of our busy lives today. One would not believe that it was once such a tranquil place. The modern St Gabriel's church stands on what was once the site of the old rectory. A number of shops once spanned the road here, selling practically everything: Papworths'; The Cabin; T.G. Cycles. Number 94 Rectory Road sold televisions, but they moved to the town centre when it opened in 1958.

PITSEA HIGH ROAD

A PHOTOGRAPH OF Pitsea High Road in 1920.
What looks like a T. Ford car can be seen. Before the
development of the town centre in 1958, most people
shopped in Pitsea, Vange or Laindon. The two former
shopping centres had ninety shops between them.
The shops started east of the rail bridge. During the
development the shops were moved down to their
present position.

There was a cinema here called The Century, which
opened in 1929. This was one of the buildings built by
local businessman Harold Howard. At that time, most
of the population went to the cinema at least twice a
week. The cinema seated 700 patrons. It was powered
by diesel generators, which were situated in a specially
built building.

The generators also provided electricity for Tudor
Chambers, the Railway Hotel, and Anne Boleyn
Mansions. They also powered the lighting in the area.
The generators were manned by the staff of the cinema
and used right up to 1956. The cinema also had live
shows, including the very popular sport, at that time, of
wrestling. *(Courtesy of Basildon Heritage Museum)*

DURING THE 1940s the cinema was taken over by Radion (Rayleigh) Ltd and then, in 1955, it was taken over by Granada, who spent £30,000 – a vast sum in those days – on renovating it, installing a Cinemascope screen, a new sound system, a restaurant and a snack bar.

They changed its name to The Century (again) and it opened, after the alterations, on 15 February 1955. In the 1960s television was becoming popular and so bingo was introduced to help the cash flow. Things came to a head in October 1970, when the last films, *Jason and the Argonauts* and *Born Free*, were shown. The building was completely converted into a bingo hall, which was the fashion at that time. Finally, it was taken over by Bass Brewery Co. and was renamed The Gala. It was closed in July 2009, and remains empty to this day.

The shopping centre, to the left of the old site, was moved to its present position in the 1960s and 1970s. The old shops were once much nearer Rectory Road. (*Courtesy of Basildon Heritage Museum*)

PITSEA POST OFFICE

PITSEA POST OFFICE in the 1940s. It was situated in the Broadway and had been there since early days. This post office served the public during the dark days of the war. After the war, when the Family Allowance Act of 1946 came into force, business must have increased. Throughout the country there were 5 million claimants. It paid out 5s for the second child and subsequent children, but none for the first. In 1952 this was increased to 8s for the second child and 10s for the third. It was not until 1977 that payment was made for the first child. Although this post office had not been built when the first penny black came out in 1840, it is a far cry from the cost of a first-class stamp today. (© *Basildon District Council*)

THE APPROXIMATE SITE of the old Pitsea post office in 2012. Tesco opened a post office in 1968 and with the pressure from them it was inevitable that the old post office would close. Tesco is open twenty-four hours a day and sells everything, and as a result the small shops that once spanned the High Street have gradually diminished. The market, which is open on a Monday, Wednesday and Saturday, attracts customers from far and wide and is helping to stem the flow and keep many of the shops alive.

ST MARGARET'S, BOWERS GIFFORD

ST MARGARET'S, Bowers Gifford, has stood on this site since Saxon times. It is thought that the first construction was of wood. A more permanent structure was built during the fourteenth century by Sir John Giffard. Traces of this building remain in the south wall and west doorway. The church was a gift of Sir John, who fought at the Battle of Crecy in 1346 with Edward III.

This was the battle in which the Black Prince won his spurs and acquired the Prince of Wales' emblem of three feathers. An estimated 7,000 English and Welsh archers played a major part in defeating the King of France, Philip VI, in northern France with their longbows. In the sanctuary is part of a brass depicting Sir John Giffard, who is shown resplendent in his armour.

Over the centuries there have been many additions to this beautiful church, including the tower, three bells and a freestanding basin for washing holy vessels. It had a major reconstruction in the sixteenth century. (*Courtesy of Basildon Heritage Museum*)

ST MARGARET'S in 2012. To reach it one has to go down a long twisty road to a railway bridge. There stands the church with its lychgate inviting one in. The tranquillity is broken occasionally by an electric train hurtling over the bridge which spans the country road. The journey is well worth making, as one passes through the peaceful countryside, away from the hustle and bustle of Basildon.

BIRD'S-EYE VIEW OF PITSEA

A BIRD'S-EYE VIEW of Pitsea in the 1930s from the cemetery at St Michael's church. This view is looking towards the Railway Tavern, which was built in 1929 by local businessman Mr Howard. Howard had a farm and set up dairies throughout Basildon. It is amazing how much development has taken place over the years. It has gone from a quiet country village to a large part of Basildon New Town. In the 1801 census the population of Pitsea was 211: today it has expanded a hundredfold.

From here, one can see for miles. In one direction is the River Crouch, Wat Tyler Country Park and the less picturesque Pitsea tip, with hundreds of seagulls scavenging amongst the rubbish. *(Courtesy of Basildon Heritage Museum)*

A SIMILAR VIEW in 2012. In the distance can be seen the Railway Tavern. The serenity of the countryside has disappeared and has been replaced by the noise of modern life. It is surprising how the trees have grown since St Michael's church went out of use, blotting out the view. Gone are many of the old shops, but up towards Rectory Road some have remained. These have modernized and sell specialist goods like computer printers, ink and tiles. What has always amazed me is that the road builders seem never to stop altering the roads in the area. It seems to have gone on for years. Will it ever stop, I wonder? Perhaps it never will.

PITSEA BROADWAY

THE PHOTOGRAPH WAS taken in the 1950s and is of the Tudor-style buildings in Pitsea. These were the work of Harold Howard, who designed them. He was a rich local farmer who set up dairies in Laindon, Pitsea and Fryerns and delivered milk by horse and cart throughout the area.

The first building he constructed in Pitsea was the Railway Hotel, followed quickly by the Tudor Chambers and Anne Boleyn Mansions. He also built a cinema in the same complex in 1929. Most families, no matter how poor, went to the cinema at least once a week. The cost was about 1*s*, but as children we did not always pay! We used to bunk in and be chased around by an usherette for the whole show.

When television took off and became available to the majority of families – on the never-never or on hire from Radio Rentals, who also ran a cable service – it became a bingo hall and changed its name to The Granada Social Club.

TUDOR BUILDINGS TODAY. Note that the war memorial is no longer there: it was moved to Howard's Park when the new development started in the 1960s. Apart from that, though, the buildings do not seem to have changed (although most of the owners of the shops have).

In the modern photograph, T. Cribb the funeral directors, who were established in 1831, dominate the front of the building. They took over from W. Newman, who, when the 1950s photograph was taken, sold garden equipment. Other shops today include a wine merchants and a café. On the left of the picture are walkways leading under the A13 to Tesco, St Michael's church, the railway station, Wat Tyler Park and Pitsea tip.

PITSEA MARKET

PITSEA MARKET STARTED its life in 1925 and was originally situated in Station Lane at the junction of Riviera Avenue. The war memorial once stood at the top of the junction until it was moved to its present position in Howard's Park. The founder of the market was the entrepreneur Charles Love. The stalls were very cheap and could be hired for as little as 1s 6d. Prominent stall holders included the Cohen brothers, who served in the market for many years and could be seen

skilfully throwing plates in the air and shouting, 'I'm not asking one pound for this fine china set, I'm not asking ten bob. Who will give me five bob?'

In 1969 the market had to be moved to make way for the road improvements to the A132 (and later the A13), which involved building the South Mayne flyover and the A13 flyover. In order to do this the developers shortened Station Lane and made it into a cul-de-sac. The market was moved to a former field on the south side of the High Road. To enable the customers to shop in comfort, they erected four purpose-built domes. These were like something out of space, and for years became a dominant feature of the Pitsea landscape. Nothing lasts for ever, however, and during the great storm of 16/17 October 1987, a cataclysm which destroyed thousands of trees and caused millions of pounds worth of damage to properties, the domes were ripped apart, as can be seen. *(Courtesy of Basildon Heritage Museum)*

THE MARKET STILL survives in 2012, despite competition from supermarkets like Tesco and Sainsbury's and, further afield, from Bluewater. It was finally moved to its present position by the side of the new shops and the Railway Tavern, and was taken over by Charfleets in the mid-1990s. It opens on Monday, Wednesday and Saturday, and one can purchase anything from the stalls, from the mundane, like rubber bands, to a birthday present for someone special. I love to wander through the vibrant stalls without any intention of buying anything – though something always catches my eye.

There are rumours that the market is on the move again in the near future, but wherever it goes I am certain it will still attract the public.

THE GUN INN

THE GUN INN, Bowers Gifford. Records show that it was first used as a public house in the eighteenth century. The first landlord was a Mr Butler. Any drunken patrons who got out of hand would be thrown into an iron cage which was conveniently located outside the public house. If they committed a more serious crime, they could be put in the stocks, which were opposite.

After the First World War, the pub gradually fell into disrepair and had to be rebuilt. After the refurbishment it held dances and sing-songs around the piano. *(Courtesy of Basildon Heritage Museum)*

THE GUN INN in March 2012. The public house of the modern era also had a somewhat tough reputation, and indeed the council eventually ordered that the pool tables be removed to prevent drinkers using the cues as clubs. They also requested that drinking glasses be unbreakable and that the establishment install CCTV and hire doormen. Pity that they still didn't have the iron cage...

Then the Gun was put up for sale. There was a proposal to demolish the public house and build flats, but the council refused planning permission. There was also a proposal to build a twenty-room hotel, but this was also refused.

I am glad to say that since Mr and Mrs Mohseni bought it there have been no complaints – only praise. It has been transformed into an excellent Persian and Mediterranean restaurant that can cater for 120 diners. It is the first public house in Basildon to obtain a twenty-four-hour licence. This was granted to prevent the owners having to apply each time for special functions.

ST MICHAEL'S CHURCH, PITSEA

ST MICHAEL'S CHURCH, Pitsea. Sadly, all that remains of this church today is the tower, which dates back to the sixteenth century. The church had been rebuilt during the nineteenth century, but it gradually fell into decline. When the church was in full use, brides had to wear Wellington boots in inclement weather when climbing the steep path to the church and had to hold on to their headdresses because of the wind. There was a custom at one time for trains to toot their whistles when they saw a wedding in the church.

There are reports – though I do not know how true these are – of farmers grazing their cattle on the hill leading up to St Michael's. Although the climb up the hill is steep, it is worth making for the view at the top – one can see the contrast between the old Pitsea and the new. (© *Basildon History Site*)

THE CHURCH WAS so small that only relations were allowed inside during large weddings: the rest of the guests had to stand outside. Unfortunately, the church fell victim to vandals and the final service took place in 1983. There were plans to turn it into a museum, but these never materialised. In 1998 the main church was demolished, leaving only the tower – on which Orange has installed a mobile mast! The tower in 2012 stands out as a symbol of days gone by as it surveys the bustling roads below. In the distance can be seen the River Crouch and Wat Tyler Park.

THE BARGE INN

THE BARGE HOUSE is believed to have been a private home at one time. The first public house on the site was called the Man with Seven Wives, as the proprietor – whose name was Mr Wives – claimed he had six wives: his wife, plus five children, made up the six.

G. Hastler, the proprietor at the time this photograph was taken, obtained his beer from the Hornchurch Brewery. The 1841 census shows that the Adey family lived at the Barge. It is understood that barge captains drank in the pub after they had moored in the River Crouch, after returning from a trip to London.

In 1848, Curtes, a brick manufacturer, had four barges – *Pitsea, Vange, Fobbing* and *Basildon* – and conveyed his goods along the river to London on them. The business was later sold to Ellis of Stanford-le-Hope.

Along the same road were many shops, including a fish and chip shop, a sweet shop, a cobbler's, a greengrocer, and a chemist. *(Image below and below right courtesy of Basildon Heritage Museum)*

THE BARGE IN February 2012. Although there is a small parade of shops behind the public house, it looks isolated, as if it is missing the company of the shops of days gone by, like Saunders the bakers (who sold crusty bread straight out of the oven). They were famous for their tasty doughnuts oozing with jam. Ernie Thorndyke did a baker's round and locals would listen out for the sound of his horse's hooves and then rush out to buy bread from the back of his horse and cart.

On the left of Timberlog Lane was Allen's Fish Shop and a café. The children were not forgotten, as they bought sherbet from the sweet shop. Opposite the Barge was Mill's the greengrocer, who was helped by his daughter Florrie – whose smile, it was said, brightened up people's lives.

CLAY HILL ROAD

CLAY HILL ROAD during the 1920s. It is difficult to imagine this quiet country road becoming the bustling road that it is today. It leads down to the Barge and on to Pitsea. During the development of the New Town the contractors used this as a shortcut and turned the road into a muddy track. Pupils on their way to school used to wait for one another and go in crocodiles to avoid being knocked down. In the 1950s the press started to call Clay Hill Road 'Nob Hill', because the houses were let to the higher income bracket. *(Courtesy of Basildon Heritage Museum)*

CLAY HILL ROAD, in 2012, has changed much since the development took place. Part of it was once called Timberlog Lane, namely the section which ran from the junction of Burnt Mills Road to the Barge in London Road. Timberlog Road was named after the carts of logs that used to travel from Basildon Forest down to the River Crouch.

Many of the minor roads in the area were mere muddy tracks just after the First World War. Many of the properties were just shacks, with no drainage: their occupants had a 'bucket and chuck it' method of disposing of waste. Most had an outdoor shed featuring a plank over a bucket; the contents would be buried every week or so. They grew wonderful tomatoes on these patches, as I can vouch for. My grandfather used the same method in his bungalow in Wickford. These properties had no running water and used filtered rain water from the roofs or from a stream if one was nearby. It was not until later on that standpipes were put in, though these had a great disadvantage: they froze in winter. For lighting, the residents used candles or paraffin lamps. To heat their properties, they again burnt paraffin, coal or logs.

REDGRAVE ROAD
AND RAVENSCOURT
DRIVE, VANGE

Nos 59, 61 AND 62 Redgrave Road is where it all started – these, and Ravenscourt Drive, Vange, can be said to be the birthplace of Basildon New Town. The first tenants started to move into the area in 1951. Two years later, No. 32 Denys Drive was the Basildon Corporation's 1,000th property. The houses were mainly built in terraces, and were far superior to the houses and flats that many of the tenants had come from.

Other Basildon housing projects, however, were less successful. By giving generous subsidies, the Government encouraged the Corporation to try new methods of building. One example

was the Blue House Estate, which was built by air being blown through concrete, rather like an aero bar. Soon after they were erected, tenants found the buildings were cracking. It must be admitted that the houses were not very popular – and that a few tenants helped the damage by dropping heavy objects, such as weights and wardrobes, on the bedroom floor. I remember being called to a house where I found the tenant sitting on the bedroom floor with his feet dangling through a hole in the sitting room's ceiling. He said the wardrobe had fallen over.

The Corporation tried various methods to prevent the external cracking, including steel bands round the houses, but to no avail. Tenants used to joke that the properties were held together with elastic bands. Eventually, in the 1990s, they were demolished, and Church View Estate was built in its place. *(Courtesy of Basildon Heritage Museum)*

A PHOTOGRAPH OF Ravenscourt Drive which was taken in approximately the same spot in 2012. The rents in those days for a two-bedroomed house ranged from £1 2s to £1 9s. Three-bedroomed houses cost £1 3s to £1 10s, and four-bedroomed houses £1 6s to £1 18s. Money was borrowed from a Government body over a period of sixty years.

Rents were subsidised by 60 per cent in the 1970s. Since the 1980 Housing Act, 28 per cent of Basildon residents took up the option to buy their own houses. They obtained them at a 60 per cent discount of the valuation, and the monies they paid went to pay off the money the Corporation had borrowed to build them.

ALL SAINTS' CHURCH, VANGE

ALL SAINTS' CHURCH, Vange. The church has some twelfth-century features, which suggest that the building may be even older than that. Wall paintings dating back to the thirteenth century can still be seen, as can some fifteenth-century windows and a seventeenth-century memorial tablet. During 1837 a gallery was added and the west wall was reconstructed. (© *Basildon History Site*)

ALL SAINTS' CHURCH, Vange. It's a pity that the church fell into disrepair – eventually it became quite dangerous. The last service was held in 1996. In view of its historical interest, however, it is cared for by the Church Conservation Trust.

In 2004 the Trust started a restoration programme, which took three years, to repair the roof and the timber inside and out of this Grade II listed building. I am glad, because it is believed to be the oldest surviving church in Basildon. It is interesting to note that at the beginning of the twentieth century the church was lit with oil lamps, which must have looked beautiful flickering on the thirteenth-century wall paintings. Although no services are held, the church is open every day between 10 a.m. and 3 p.m. and is well worth a visit.

FORD'S TRACTOR FACTORY

FORD'S TRACTOR FACTORY started construction in 1957 on the land which was Oliphant's Farm. In the seventeenth century the farm was owned by a physician to James I, Dr Henry Althums. Ford's tractors were exported all over the world and it was one of the biggest employers in Basildon. It was taken over in 1998 by New Holland Tractor Plant, which is owned by Fiat, an

Italian firm. They continued to build tractors and employ a large number of personnel from the surrounding area. Men who worked on the assembly line said it paid good money but was hard work. They alleged that the belt speed was increased so that they had to work harder to keep up, especially at night. Discipline was strict, and if you committed three offences you were sacked. (© *Ford*)

ORD   MOTOR   COMPANY   LTD.
ASILDON   TRACTOR   PLANT
roject   No: Y/8
onsultant :   Artek   (UK)   LTD.
ontractor :   G.   P.   Trentham
iew :   As   Indicated
ate : 6.6.63.   Photo   No.

BASILDON DEVELOPMENT CORPORATION leased the land to manufacturers for a period of between 99 and 999 years at £250 per acre. They would either build the factory or the firm would do so themselves. The advantages of setting up a business in Basildon were that rents, rates and land were cheaper. There were also good transport connections (although Basildon Station had not been built at that time). There was a large workforce in the area waiting to be trained. Although Ford's no longer own the factory, New Holland Tractors do. The tractor plant has manufactured 1.8 million machines and exports them to 120 countries all around the world. In the factory (and I find this difficult to imagine) they have 2km of assembly lines. New Holland is a very old established firm which commenced trading in Holland in 1895.

YARDLEY'S
FACTORY

YARDLEY'S FACTORY DURING the 1960s. Yardley's was one
of the oldest cosmetic companies in the world: it began when a
member of the Yardley family offered Charles I an unspecified sum
of money for a concession to manufacture soap for the whole of
London. By 1770 they had branched out into perfumes and were
being run by William Cleaver, who had married into the family.
He got into financial trouble and the firm reverted to the Yardleys,
who set up a factory in London.

In 1921 it branched out in America and became a limited
company. After the Second World War they advertised their
lipsticks by calling them 'women's ammunition'.

In 1960, they took advantage of the generous deal that
Basildon Corporation offered and set up a factory in Basildon, at
No. 2 Industrial Estate at Pipps Hill. They were one of the biggest
employers in the area. They manufactured lipstick, perfumes,
face powder and all types of cosmetics. Pat Radley, who worked

there, told me that the assembly belt started up directly they got through the door in the morning. The girls would sit on either side of a moving belt, packing the produce. If they could not keep up with the pace of the belt, the cosmetics would fall through a hole and they had to deal with them when the belt broke down, which was frequently. As employers they were very strict and would only allow staff five minutes to go to the toilet – though they did provide a staff restaurant, social club, tennis courts and football pitch. Gavin Williams, who worked for Yardley's for seventeen years and was there at the end, said, 'They were good employers and looked after their staff.'

THE SITE OF Yardley's in 2012. Their factory was given a Royal Institute of British Architecture award for its modern design. Unfortunately, the firm went into liquidation in 1998 and was auctioned off over 21 and 22 April 1999 in 2,000 lots. Items auctioned included office furniture, computers and packing machines. The German firm Wella bought the name, and so the name of Yardley lives on.

BASILDON ARTS CENTRE

FOR A LONG time the population of Basildon campaigned for its own theatre. Local groups such as Laindon Players and The Talian Theatre Group were very good, and put on plays and musicals, but the residents wanted somewhere to host names of national and international importance too. Finally, in 1968, a temporary building was erected which could hold an audience of 500. It was opened by the chairman of The Arts Council of Great Britain, Lord Goodman. It later became the Towngate Theatre and was the first purpose-built arts centre in the UK. It put on operas, dance, drama, pantomime and films. It had studios for painting, pottery and photography. My own two sons attended pottery classes in the 1970s. The studios doubled for rehearsals for amateur groups. It closed when the new theatre opened in April 1988.

The Festival Hall opened in 1982 and could seat 1,000 people. They held concerts and boxing events. It was built on the site of the old Basildon Zoo. It fell victim to the Festival Park and was demolished only eight years after it was built. (© *Basildon District Council*)

ST MARTIN'S SQUARE in 2012. On the left of the picture is the new Towngate Theatre. The rest of the picture shows the Town Hall and library. Departments of the council previously worked from Freedom House and a wooden building which they shared with the library. The square was opened in 1997 by Local Government and Housing Minister Hilary Armstrong, MP. A competition was held to name the square. Lee Clart, aged eleven, and Laura Anderson, aged nine, won it by calling the square St Martin's, which seems to capture the tranquillity of the area and gives it a Continental feel.

To the right of the picture is Church House, which was purpose-built for the Commission for New Towns to house many of its housing functions, including senior staff, lettings and rebates. There was, at first, one Basildon Council cashier and a Welfare Rights department. Later, the two organisations shared the building until the Commission was wound up.

THE
FIVE BELLS

A PUBLIC HOUSE has been on this site for
centuries, supplying travellers with refreshments
as they journeyed from London on the old A13.
The first recorded landlord was William West,
here in 1769. One of the waitresses whispered in
my ear that the pub had a ghost, a figure dressed
in old-fashioned clothes who has been seen (and
heard) gliding around the rooms. Twinned with
The Five Bells was The Old Forge, which served
the local community of farmers, shoeing their
horses and repairing their wagons. The Old Forge
is mentioned as far back as the seventeenth
century. The public house could have been a
staging post on the journey from London to
Southend. *(Courtesy of Basildon Heritage Museum)*

THE FIVE BELLS in 2012. The public house is now a Harvester Restaurant, but still retains that look of years gone by, inside and out. It is a favourite public house for ramblers and families who have experienced the beauty of Laindon Hills and want to relax in comfortable surroundings and enjoy a good meal.

The Old Forge no longer shares the site, having gone in the 1950s. Despite the busy A13 road running close by, the public house retains the tranquillity it must have had in centuries past.

ST MARY'S
AND ALL
SAINTS'

ST MARY'S AND ALL SAINTS' was built in 1877
on the foundations of a previous church. It
replaced the previous St Mary's, which is in Old
Church Hill and was sold in 1970 and converted
into a private house. The list of its priests goes back
to 1366. The first priest of this church was Will
De Swafeild, and the last recorded priest was Cecil
Livesey in 1930. There are two bells, weighing
3cwt and 1cwt. The larger of these has two
crosses and a shield engraved on it. It was made,
as many church bells were made, in Aldgate by the
bell-maker Thomas Lawrence. There are a number
of tombstones in the church, and one dates back to
the fourteenth century. This one is of marble and

shows signs that at one time it had brasses inset in it. There are two grave-slabs set in the floor of the chancel which have inscriptions in Old English. One is the grave of Elizabeth Richardson, who was the wife of Thomas Richardson.

The altar rail is made of oak and could date back to the seventeenth century. *(Courtesy of Basildon Heritage Museum)*

ST MARY'S AND ALL SAINTS' is now in a beautiful spot, surrounded by trees. It is not far from the Crown Hotel, where the first recorded landlady was Mary Waldon in 1828.

Outside, on the face of the church's south-east buttress, is a mark 18in above the ground, which indicates that the point is 211ft above sea level. Laindon Hills, just a short distance down the road, are 387ft above sea level, the second highest point in Essex. Who ever said that Essex is flat?!

VANGE SCHOOL

VANGE SCHOOL IS one of the oldest schools in Basildon, having been opened in 1876. During the 1900s the school was enlarged and later an extension was built. Another school stood nearby, but it was demolished – and Basildon Zoo was built on the site. The zoo has now closed. At one time traffic on the A13 roared past, but this all changed when, in the 1970s, the A13 was diverted and the Vange and Pitsea bypass opened.

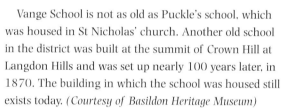

Vange School is not as old as Puckle's school, which was housed in St Nicholas' church. Another old school in the district was built at the summit of Crown Hill at Langdon Hills and was set up nearly 100 years later, in 1870. The building in which the school was housed still exists today. *(Courtesy of Basildon Heritage Museum)*

THE VANGE SCHOOL today has only 123 pupils, aged between three and eleven years old. I wonder how the education children receive today compares to the time when the school first opened? The discipline would certainly have been stricter in those far-off days, with behaviour being governed by the fear of the cane. Children tried all kinds of methods to alleviate the pain, such as rubbing orange peel on their palms before the caning, or holding their hands down in the hope that the cane would slide off. I can vouch that none of them worked.

If you enjoyed this book, you may also be interested in…

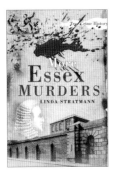

More Essex Murders

LINDA STRATMANN

From the pretty villages, rural byways and bustling market towns of Essex come ten of the most dramatic and tragic murder cases in British history. Brutality, passion, jealousy, greed and moments of inexplicable rage have led to violent and horrifying deaths and, sometimes, the killer's expiation of the crime on the scaffold. This chilling follow-up to *Essex Murders* brings together more true cases, dating between 1823 and 1960, that shocked not only the county but also made headline news across the nation.

978 0 7524 5850 2

Paranormal Essex

JASON DAY

A tour around one of England's oldest and most paranormally active counties. Visit the site of the 'Most Haunted House in England' at Borley, encounter the mysterious Spider of Stock, witness an RAF pilot's shocking near miss with a UFO over the skies of Southend, and find out how the infamous 'Witchfinder General' served as judge, jury and executioner in Manningtree. With accounts of hauntings, monsters, UFOs, Big Cats, and more, *Paranormal Essex* will delight all lovers of the unexplained.

978 0 7524 5527 3

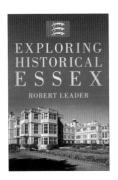

Exploring Historical Essex

ROBERT LEADER

This engaging book paints a comprehensive picture of Essex; bringing the reader on an exploratory journey from Brightlingsea to Wivenhoe whilst uncovering the secrets and history this fine county has to offer. Serving as both an inspiring guide and a lasting souvenir, this book is richly illustrated with the author's photographs, bringing historical Essex to life.

978 0 7524 5764 2

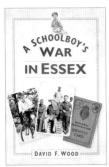

A Schoolboy's War in Essex

DAVID F. WOOD

Although only children at the time, the Second World War had a permanent effect on the schoolboys who lived through the conflict. Watching a country preparing for war and then being immersed in the horrors of the Blitz brought encounters and events that some will never forget. Now in their seventies and eighties, many are revisiting their memories of this period for the first time. In this charming book, David F. Wood recalls his days as a schoolboy in Essex, where his family moved when the Luftwaffe threatened his native London.

978 0 7524 5517 4

Visit our website and discover thousands of other History Press books.

www.thehistorypress.co.uk